LOVE
Yourself
BIG

A GUIDE FOR WOMEN
WHO GIVE TOO MUCH

*Prioritize Your Well-Being, Practice
Self-Care & Purge Toxic Energy*

MICHELLE KULP

Copyright © 2020 by **Monarch Crown Publishing**

Expanded Edition. All Rights Reserved. No part of this book may be reproduced in any form without permission in writing from the author. Reviewers may quote brief passages in reviews.
ISBN: 978-1-7340538-7-6

This book is designed to provide accurate and authoritative information in regard to the subject matter herein. It is sold with the understanding that the author and publisher is not engaged in rendering legal, accounting, or other professional services. If you require legal advice or other expert assistance, you should seek the services of a competent professional.

While the author has made every effort to provide accurate website addresses and other information at the time of publication, neither the publisher nor the author assumes any responsibility for errors or changes that occur after publication. Further, the publisher does not have any control over and does not assume any responsibility for author or third-party websites or their content.

TABLE OF CONTENTS

SIGNS YOU MAY BE AN OVER-GIVER 1

THE ANTIDOTE FOR WOMEN WHO GIVE TOO MUCH 3

THE STORY OF THE ORPHANED LAMB 5

MY STORY 7

CHAPTER 1: CREATING YOUR ABSOLUTE NO & ABSOLUTE YES LIST 13

CHAPTER 2: REMOVING 25% OF WHAT IS ON YOUR PLATE 19

CHAPTER 3: BEGIN EVERY DAY WITH 3 ACTS OF SELF-CARE 29

CHAPTER 4: CREATING A SOUL-NOURISHING ENVIRONMENT 37

CHAPTER 5: 10 LAWS OF BOUNDARIES FOR WOMEN WHO GIVE TOO MUCH 49

CHAPTER 6: OVERCOMING THE DISEASE TO PLEASE 61

CHAPTER 7: DON'T SAY YES, WHEN YOU WANT TO SAY NO 67

CHAPTER 8: TAG YOU'RE IT! LEARNING TO ASK FOR HELP 71

CHAPTER 9: PROTECTING YOUR ENERGY FROM TOXIC PEOPLE 79

CHAPTER 10: PRIORITZING SELF CARE IN TO YOUR SCHEDULE 87

CLOSING THOUGHTS 91

Dear Over-Giver,

It's time.

It's time for a time-out on giving to others.

Giving is good when it comes from a place of fullness, completeness, and self-love.

However, this type of over-giving is coming from a place of lack and unworthiness, which is creating physical, emotional, mental and spiritual exhaustion.

It's time to clear the space and make room to prioritize your own self-care, well-being and fulfillment.

It's time for a "TIME IN."

You learned a long time ago (or so you thought) that the more you gave, the more people would love you, accept you, admire you, appreciate you, and that they would give you the same level of unconditional generosity that you gave to them.

The only problem is, it's not working.

You're trying to be Super-Woman to everyone by playing multiple roles such as:

- Super-Mom
- Super-Grandma
- Super-Wife
- Super-Partner
- Super-Friend

- Super-Sibling
- Super-Housekeeper
- Super-Cook
- Super-Caretaker
- Super-Daycare Provider
- Super-Employee
- Super-Business Owner
- Super-Social Organizer
- Super-Giver to Philanthropic Organizations
- Super-Gift Giver
- Super Holiday Host
- Super-Email Responder
- Super-Social Media Person

And the list goes on and on.

The problem with being a super-giver and playing multiple roles that are all based on giving to others is – IT'S DRAINING YOU!

You're exhausted, depleted, resentful, angry, unhappy at times, unfulfilled, unappreciated, worn-out, and irritated; you know deep inside it has to stop.

The path you are on is the direct path to BURNOUT; which is now a medical diagnosis given by the World Health Organization.

Being an over-giver is not only a bad habit, it's an addiction. It may have started with good intentions to "help others" and to be a "good person," but it has slowly (over time) turned dysfunctional and is rooted in an unmet need to feel "worthy," take up space in the world and to feel like you matter.

You've been receiving messages your entire life that your worthiness is based on what you can do for others. As the saying goes, *"What have you done for me lately?"*

The world and the people in your life will happily continue to accept your over-giving because that means they don't have to step up and take care of themselves, be accountable, grow up, be mature adults and take care of their responsibilities.

They have YOU to do it for them.

Sometimes over-giving manifests as giving yourself to philanthropy or to your work in the name of service; but giving more to others than you give to yourself has created an imbalance.

It's time for you to give up your role as *"QUEEN OVER-GIVER"* and take a step back. When you STOP giving to others from a place of lack, you will begin to feel the emptiness inside that you've been hiding from and avoiding.

You can't deprive yourself of oxygen any longer; it's life and death.

Signed,

Your Inner *"Self-Care"* Sage

SIGNS YOU MAY BE AN OVER-GIVER

- You live in a chronic state of resentment because you do so much for others that you don't have time to do things for yourself.
- Your relationships do not have an equal amount of give and take and are more rooted in what you have to offer and give to others.
- You have fantasies of running away from home to escape your stressed-out life.
- You rarely take a vacation that is YOU-centered.
- You have a hard time asking for help.
- You play the *Good Girl* role and never want to disappoint others.
- You feel like the world will fall apart if you don't keep giving and doing what you're doing.
- You avoid hurting other people's feelings at the expense of your own.
- You do not like confrontation and avoid it at all costs.
- You don't express your emotions.
- You suck it up and do what needs to be done.
- You never take time for yourself.
- You complain that no one appreciates you.
- You feel deprived.
- You have a pattern of self-neglect.

- You are sleep deprived.
- You neglect your health.
- You neglect your finances.
- You don't set clear boundaries with others.
- Toxic people have full access to you.
- Your house is cluttered and in disarray.
- Your life is chaotic and overscheduled.
- You take on high-maintenance clients.
- You don't know how to separate work from your personal life.
- You feel guilty when you try to set boundaries.
- People tend to take advantage of your goodness.
- You send mixed messages to people.
- You expect people to read your mind and know what you need.
- You break promises to yourself.
- You are not living your dream life.
- You have no hobbies or healthy outlets.
- You secretly want to be acknowledged for everything you do for others.

GUIDELINES FOR WOMEN WHO GIVE TOO MUCH

1. We create our 'Absolute NO' and our 'Absolute YES' list; we review these daily.

2. We remove 25% of what is currently on our plates.

3. We start our day with three acts of self-care (from the Master Self-Care list).

4. We create a soul-nourishing work and home environment.

5. We set clear boundaries with others.

6. We prioritize and schedule self-care acts into our schedule.

7. We practice saying NO to requests of our time and give ourselves a 24-hour buffer to respond to requests.

8. We stop playing the good girl and people pleaser roles.

9. We proactively protect our energy from others.

10. We regularly ask for help.

11. We remove and/or put limits on toxic people in our lives.

12. We give ourselves permission to disappoint others.

THE STORY OF THE ORPHANED LAMB

At the Apricot Lane Farm owned by John and Molly Chester, there was an orphaned lamb that was rejected by its community and struggled to connect despite its empathy and goodness.

The orphaned lamb's mother died a few days after its birth leaving the lamb hungry and in search of a new mom. When the orphaned lamb's basic needs could not be met, he had to look beyond what was in front of him.

The orphaned lamb went searching for comfort and food; he wanted to be comforted by anything. He was desperate and repeatedly attempted to get other mother lambs to feed him, but they all rejected him because he was not their own.

The orphaned lamb did not give up though; he was determined to get fed.

One day, the orphaned lamb decided to stand behind one of the mother lambs to get fed (instead of in front of her like he usually did) and quickly realized that as long as she could not see him, she was accepting of the orphaned lamb.

The orphaned lamb was finally fed because he did not give up; he persevered.

Once the orphaned lamb stopped chasing the flock that was incapable of seeing him, he could find food and nourishment.

The orphaned lamb flourished and was finally embraced into the flock and the community at the farm.

An instinct emerged, like a whisper in the orphan lamb's ear, that said:

"Nourish yourself and the world will be drawn to you."

The story of the Orphaned Lamb is from Oprah's *Super Soul Sunday* minis, and teaches the universal lesson that we all must *learn to nourish ourselves and when we do, then we will be fed.*

Erich Fromm, a well-known psychologist once said, "*The main task in life is to give birth to our self, to become what we actually are.*"

MY STORY

After working in a fast-paced work environment in the legal field for 17 years, one day, life as I knew it abruptly stopped.

The law firm I was working at gave me the pink slip and my entire identity, which was my job title, schedule, relationships, paycheck, benefits, and more, disappeared.

It felt like DEATH.

A death of everything I was. My entire identity fell apart. and that "falling apart" landed me in the emergency room when I thought I was having a heart attack.

After an EKG and some other tests, the doctors couldn't find anything "physically" wrong with me, so they started asking me questions about my "stress" levels. I told them I didn't have any stress in my life (which was far from the truth). I actually didn't realize I had so much stress until I started talking about the current state of my life:

- I was fired from my job at the law firm.

- I was living paycheck-to-paycheck.

- I had no savings.

- My landlord gave me notice to move out or buy the house I was living in, but I didn't have the means to do so.

- I was divorced and raising three young children on my own.

- My older brother and best friend, Michael, was diagnosed with AIDS and was dying.

- Even though I was burnt out in the legal field, I didn't know how else to support myself.

- I quit drinking alcohol (which had been numbing my emotions for years) and now I was overwhelmed with them.

- My ex-husband wasn't paying child support and I was in a constant court battle with him.

- I felt lost and confused about my future.

- I was physically, mentally, spiritually and emotionally drained.

Once the doctors inquired about these details, they determined I didn't have a physical problem; I had a mental health problem. The diagnosis: panic attacks.

It felt like I had been on a hamster wheel going 100 mph when the wheel suddenly stopped. That's when the panic attacks began.

The doctors wanted to prescribe medication for the panic attacks, except there was one big problem. I had been an "anti-medication" person my entire life and did not want to take prescription pills. I asked them if there was an alternative, and they said NO.

I decided I would not take the prescribed medication; instead, I went to the bookstore looking for another way to deal with these panic attacks and stress.

Thankfully, I found a book on meditation called *Wherever You Go, There You Are* by Jon KabatZinn. That book saved my life.

Within a short time, my panic attacks disappeared. I often tell people I chose "meditation over medication."

In the spirit of transparency, I am not a trained counselor, psychologist or therapist – although I have had several great therapists over the years and have done a lot of spiritual and emotional healing work. This book is simply what I've learned on my journey towards wholeness, healing, self-love and self-acceptance.

Every time I thought I was done doing the deep emotional work, new situations came up that revealed another layer of healing was needed. And, ironically, these were always situations I couldn't run away from or sweep under the rug.

Many energy workers say that until we heal the pain and trauma, we keep repeating the same thing over and over and over. When we choose to do the deep work, we often come back around to those situations, but this time at a higher level of consciousness and awareness.

Marianne Williamson, talked about this in her book, *A Return to Love*, with this analogy:

> *"When you're really ill, you don't even know a snake when you see one. Once recovery begins, you see a snake, but you still play with it. Once you've landed in the true recovery zone, you see a snake, you know it's a snake, and you cross to the other side of the road."*

In her book, she was talking about recovering from relationships with toxic men, but this story shows our level of consciousness in all things.

Level 1 – Completely Unaware

Level 2 – Somewhat Aware, But Not Healed

Level 3 – Conscious and Healed

During those 17 years in the legal field and dealing with the ups and downs of life, I was in Level 1. It wasn't until I had the space in my life (getting fired from the law firm) that I began to explore and become more aware; then I moved to Level 2.

Level 3 is what we all aspire to – being completely conscious of our choices and healed.

I've always needed outside help to see past my blind spots, and I've met some excellent health practitioners along the way, which I will share with you in the resources section of this book. These healers transformed and saved my life.

Since you picked up this book on loving yourself, overcoming over-giving, practicing self-care, prioritizing your well-being and purging toxic energy, I know you are at Level 2. You are aware, which is a great place to be.

Life coach, speaker, talk show host, and bestselling author of the book, *The 5-Second Rule*, Mel Robbins, says:

"If you have a problem that can be fixed by action, then you really don't have a problem."

That's great news because I have a lot of *action* steps in this book that you can take to put yourself at the top of the list of people you love, take care of and respect.

Practicing self-care takes time to implement. This is not a one-and-done event. You *practice* self-care until it becomes your norm.

Bestselling Author and Life Coach, Cheryl Richardson, says,

"A high quality life has more to do with what you remove from it, than what you add to it."

A lot of this book is about removing what is blocking you from living a joyful and peaceful life and then adding self-care routines and rituals so you can stay in the healthy zone. The medical field has a term for – "homeostasis" – which means a state of equilibrium.

In order to be in that state of equilibrium, we must start nourishing ourselves – like the orphaned lamb did. It's not an option; it's a requirement.

When you start on the path towards prioritizing your well-being, think of it like using training wheels. The more you do it, the better you get at it until one day you can take the training wheels off and self-care will become your norm.

I listed the *Guidelines for Women Who Give Too Much* above, and each chapter expands on those solutions. I also have a **SELF-CARE MASTER LIST** that includes actions you can choose from and incorporate into your life on a daily basis.

I'm writing this book to myself as well, as I've struggled with the nice girl syndrome, over-giving, neglecting my self-care, and being a people pleaser my entire life.

I'm excited you're taking this journey with me, so let's get started…

CHAPTER 1: CREATING YOUR "ABSOLUTE NO" AND "ABSOLUTE YES" LIST

I had finally ended an eight-year relationship with a man who cheated on me. It was hard to do, but with the help of a great therapist, I did it. The problem was I always went back. This time, however, I wanted it to "stick," which is why I started seeing a therapist.

My therapist said that when it comes to relationships, many women suffer from *amnesia* and over time we "forget" the bad things in the relationship and only remember the good things. She suggested I write a list of all the bad things in that relationship and then, when I started missing my ex (and had amnesia), I should pull out the list and read it.

I'm happy to say it worked! I can't tell you how many times over the next year I pulled out that list. It prevented me from going into that *"I miss him so much"* state of mind and calling him. The list saved me from getting back into a very unhealthy and toxic relationship.

I love lists! Lists allow us to keep things in the forefront of our minds instead of buried beneath the busy-ness of our lives.

This chapter details how to create two lists that will help guide you on your path to prioritizing your well-being—your ABSOLUTE NO and your ABSOLUTE YES lists.

- **ABSOLUTE NO LIST** – What you will NOT tolerate in your life – from yourself and from others.

- **ABSOLUTE YES LIST** – What you are committing to taking care of – including yourself.

You can start with either list. I'm going to start here with the **ABSOLUTE NO list**.

Here's what is on my list:

- I will NOT automatically say yes to requests anymore. When people request something of me such as helping them, going somewhere, or being a part of something – I will say, "*Thank you so much for thinking of me. I'll check my schedule and get back to you.*" Then, I will use the 24-hour rule and meditate on that request. I will see how my body feels about it when I think of doing it and whether I really want to do it. I no longer do things out of obligation or guilt.

- I will NOT give people who are narcissists, chronic complainers, and who have a high amount of negative and toxic energy access to myself. If I can't completely remove them from my life, I will minimize my time with them.

- I will NOT do things for others who are capable of doing those things for themselves, even if it means being uncomfortable and feeling bad for a short time. I will clearly tell others I'm NOT taking care of their responsibilities.

- I will NOT let people suck my energy from me. I will protect my energy and will use my sacred bubble exercise in my meditation daily.

CREATING YOUR ABSOLUTE NO & ABSOLUTE YES LIST

- I will NOT let others infringe on my morning routine. Therefore, I will not respond to calls, emails, texts or any interruptions during my morning routine.
- I will NOT allow others to block my writing time.
- I will NOT do things I don't want to do out of obligation or guilt.
- I will NOT date unhealthy men.
- I will NOT take on high-maintenance clients and I will pay attention to the red flags.

Now it's your turn to write your ABSOLUTE NO list. What will you NOT tolerate from yourself and others? Write at least 10 items on your list.

Now it's time for the ABSOLUTE YES list. This is about what you are committing to taking care of.

Here's my list:

- I will take care of my health by getting an annual physical and going twice a year for dental cleanings.
- I will do a three-mile walk every day; a 30 minute personal training session weekly; and yoga three times per week.
- I will take care of my spiritual self by doing my morning routine every day which includes: meditation, journaling, gratitude list and spiritual reading.

- I will take care of my house and keep everything organized, clean and decorated in a way that inspires me and brings me joy.

- I will take care of my finances and set up automatic payments for my bills so I don't have to waste time and energy thinking about or wondering if I paid a bill.

- I will take care of my taxes in a timely manner.

- I will continue to save money so I always have enough in the bank to pay my living expenses for two years.

- I will say YES to requests after the 24-hour rule has been implemented and only if I really want to do that request.

- I will say YES to healthy men who want to get to know me slowly and who respect me.

- I will say YES to spending time in nature every day, especially, in the sun for my Vitamin D levels.

- I will say YES to my writing time and protect it as sacred time.

- I will say YES to Divine orders.

- I will say YES to working with great clients and helping them get their books out to the world!

- I will say YES to spending time with my family and healthy friends.

CREATING YOUR ABSOLUTE NO & ABSOLUTE YES LIST · 17

> Now it's your turn to write your **ABSOLUTE YES** list. What will you absolutely take care of in your life? If you are a parent with children living at home, have a significant other, have a business or job, include those. Write at least 10 items on your list.

It's important to write these lists and review them daily. We all have great intentions, but not so great follow through. In other words, we suffer from amnesia.

The "little things" in life are easy to do, but they are also easy not to do. Even though our lives have been a certain way for a long time, and those ways aren't working any longer, it's hard to implement new habits and changes.

Having your **Absolute No** and **Absolute Yes** list will be a gentle reminder for you every day to prioritize your well-being.

If you need to, tape it up on your bathroom mirror so you see it when you wake up every day or place it somewhere that makes sense for you so you won't forget about it.

I promise that if you read these two lists daily, your life will begin to shift.

I put my lists in a special place where I do my morning routine every day!

CHAPTER 2: REMOVING 25% OF WHAT IS ON YOUR PLATE

*"One does not accumulate but eliminate.
It is not daily increase, but daily decrease.
The height of cultivation always runs to simplicity."
~ Bruce Lee*

In 2020, I decided I was going to write a book each month. Writing is my passion. I've been running my online business, www.bestsellingauthorprogram.com since January of 2013 and I love helping authors get their books out to the world in a BIG way!

For the last few years, I found myself complaining that I didn't have "time" to work on my own books because I was taking care of all my clients' books.

Writing a book a month is a huge undertaking, and in order to stick to my goal, I had to remove a lot of things from my life. Here is some of what I removed:

- Long and frequent phone calls from family and friends
- Mindless TV
- Reading books (Note: I love reading books, but if I'm doing a lot of reading, then I'm not writing)
- Responding quickly to every text message or email
- Too much time on Facebook
- Cleaning time (I hired a cleaning company)

Writing a book a month required me to remove these time-suckers so I could have more of it to write. Also, writing a book a month requires a lot of down time for me to mentally prepare to write the book, so I needed to spend more time in nature and going for walks.

Most of our lives are over-scheduled, busy and chaotic.

Tim Ferris, author of *The 4-Hour Work Week,* says this about being busy:

"Being busy is most often used as a guise for avoiding the few critically important but uncomfortable actions."

I believe people aren't living their dream lives because they are busy and don't want to do the uncomfortable actions.

In order to prioritize your well-being, you absolutely must start removing things in your life that will give you back your time and essentially your life.

TIME AUTOPSY

The first step is to perform a TIME AUTOPSY to see where your time is going. The purpose of the time autopsy is not to judge where your time goes, but to simply be an observer. People say all the time, "I don't have the time to do _____" (their dream) or "I don't have the time for self-care." Of course, you don't have the time; that's because you're over-giving to everyone and everything. It's time to pull back the curtain just like Dorothy did in the *Wizard of Oz* and see clearly where your time is going.

One thing I've also discovered is when we are doing things we DON'T really want to be doing, it drains our energy levels and our spirits, so we don't feel like doing the things we really want to do.

To get control of your time, you are going to do your own TIME AUTOPSY.

> **THE 3-STEP TIME AUTOPSY**
>
> 1. Spend one full week charting where your time goes. Use a calendar, a journal, a notepad, or your online calendar and start tracking everything you do during the week.
>
> 2. Review the chart at the end of that week and circle the things you can remove right now. Don't try to remove everything. Use a green highlighter to mark things you want to take off your list.
>
> 3. Over time, you will want to remove more things; the goal is to remove 25% of what is on your plate right now. Use a yellow highlighter to mark things you will work on removing to free up your time in the near future.

When it comes to time management, almost every business coach I've ever worked with has suggested I track where I was spending my time in my business so I could get control of it. I often discovered I was doing $10/hour work instead of focusing on my core competencies and strengths. I had to learn to outsource and stop trying to do everything by myself in my business.

Julia Cameron, in her book, *The Artists Way*, talks about recovering our creativity, and one of the exercises in her book is called *Reading Deprivation*. I am someone who could read a book a day if I had the time, so the thought of reading deprivation for a week was not a pleasant one. Here's what Julia says about it:

> *"Reading deprivation is a very powerful tool – and a very frightening one. Even thinking about it can bring up enormous rage. For most blocked creatives, reading is an addiction. We gobble up the words of others rather than digest our own thoughts and feelings; rather than cook up something of our own."*

Maybe "reading" isn't your addiction, maybe it's Netflix or talking on the phone for hours or scrolling on social media – we all have things we can remove in our lives that will bring us closer to our goals.

Tim Ferris says, *"Effectiveness is doing the things that get you closer to your goals."*

Your #1 goal right now is prioritizing your well-being and implementing daily acts of self-care. In order to do that, you'll have to start removing things in your life that are sucking away your time.

In his book, *Deep Work*, author Cal Newport says, *"Clarity about what matters provides clarity about what does not."*

The things that are sucking away your life are small, little insidious things that have to do with the 24/7 technology world that we live in.

Right now, as I'm working on this chapter, there is a business webinar I wanted to attend. However, finishing this chapter and staying on task to meet my deadline is more important. Hopefully, there will be a replay. I find that I'm always balancing "consuming content" with "creating content." I love reading, researching, getting on webinars, and listening to podcasts; however, if I do that too much, then I remove the time I could be using to create my own content – like this book or a new online course or blog post or my own podcast. That's the trade-off we all face.

Let's say Facebook is a big time sucker for you. If I asked you what benefits you got from spending 12 hours last week on Facebook, what would you say?

About a year ago, I was attending a book festival with my father and I came upon the book, *How to Break Up With Your Phone*, by Catherine Price. I loved the title and bought the book with the intention of giving it to my adult children who I thought had a problem with spending too much time on their phones. Turns out, after reading it, I discovered that I had a problem and I needed to break up with my phone.

I didn't realize how much time I was spending online under the "guise" of research, learning, etc. I quickly implemented the 30-day plan for the phone break up. I'm happy to tell you the author of the book is not encouraging people to cut all ties with technology; she is helping you become more aware of your technology addiction and get it under control.

Think about this: "Just as drugs have become more powerful over time, so has the thrill of behavioral feedback. Product designers are smarter than ever. They know how to push our buttons and how to encourage us to use their products, not just once but over and over." ~Adam Alter, *Irresistible: The Rise of Addictive Technology and the Business of Keeping Us Hooked*

Let's look at some statistics about technology from her Catherine Price's book:

- Americans check their phones about 47 times per day. For people between 18 and 24, the average is 82. Collectively, this adds up to more than nine billion phone checks every day.

- On average, Americans spend more than four hours a day on their phones. That amounts to about 28 hours a week, 112 hours a month, or 56 full days a year.

So when people say they don't have time for self-care, I would look to technology as the number one or two blocker of your time.

I hear all the time that being on social media (or their choice of technology) helps people relax, but actually it doesn't. There are many negative side effects to our brain by being over-connected to our phones and to technology. I'm not going to get into all the details; you can read *How to Break Up with Your Phone* for more information.

My goal is to help you see where your time is going, so you can add it back in to your self-care routine.

Our time is being sucked away one email, one text, one Facebook post, one Instagram story at a time. It seems harmless at first, but it's sinister and can take over our lives.

I have a good friend who is not on any social media, however, she does have a vice and that is the Hallmark channel and romance books. She spends all of her "free" time watching these shows and reading these books and is short on time for self-care and doing things that bring her joy.

We weren't meant to sit around all day and watch Netflix and stare at the TV or our phones. I have created a **Master Self-Care list**, which I share later in this book so you can start adding these things into your daily routine.

> Once you've done your "Time Autopsy," it's time to make some cuts. Make a list of 10 things you are going to remove or cut back on in your life.

After I read Catherine Price's book, here are some changes I made that freed up more of my time:

- I now get on Facebook twice a day for 10 minutes at a time and set a timer.
- I don't open my emails first thing in the morning; I do my morning routine and my writing instead.
- I balance my addiction to consumption by limiting webinars to twice per week and watching the replays if I'm busy doing my self-care or writing.

- I cleaned out the apps on my phone – removed those I wasn't using and put only apps that were not time wasters on my home page.

- I have a tracking app on my phone so I know how much time I spend on my phone and on which specific apps.

- I do not get on my phone two hours before bedtime.

- I do not get on my phone for one hour after waking up.

- I keep my phone on vibrate and allow myself to answer messages within 24-48 hours. I refuse to be on call to the world, so I give myself breathing room.

- I turned off all notifications.

- I have a technology-free day at least one time per week.

- I always keep my phone in another room when I am doing deep work such as writing books.

I thought it was important to include this section on technology because I believe it is sucking up our time with very low or no benefits.

When you start becoming aware and removing your go-to time wasters, you'll find plenty of time for prioritizing your self-care acts.

Here's a list of things that may be sucking your time:

- Doing things for others they could be doing for themselves

- Being on call for work 24/7 and not having a work/personal life separation or balance

- Over Volunteering
- Over Giving
- Over Scheduling
- FOMO — Fear of Missing Out
- Being busy, but not effective
- Technology – emails, social media, text messages, phone calls, etc.
- Worrying
- Over Watching the news or political shows or mindless TV
- Drama
- Toxic People

I'm sure there are other things I haven't thought of, but once you do your own time autopsy, you'll have a very clear picture of where your time goes and how to reclaim it.

Now that you've done some clearing work, let's begin to add some self-care acts into your life.

CHAPTER 3: BEGIN EVERY DAY WITH THREE ACTS OF SELF-CARE

Did you ever see the movie, *What About Bob?*, with Bill Murray? It's one of my favorite movies.

Here's the storyline from the website, IMDb:

"Doctor Leo Marvin, an egotistical psychotherapist in New York City, is looking forward to his forthcoming appearance on a "Good Morning America" telecast, during which he plans to brag about "Baby Steps," his new book about emotional disorder theories in which he details his philosophy of treating patients and their phobias. Meanwhile, Bob Wiley is a recluse who is so afraid to leave his own apartment that he has to talk himself out the door. When Bob is pawned off on Leo by a psychotherapist colleague, Bob becomes attached to Leo. Leo finds Bob extremely annoying. When Leo accompanies his wife Fay, his daughter Anna, and his son Siggy to a peaceful New Hampshire lakeside cottage for a month-long vacation, Leo thinks he's been freed from Bob. Leo expects to mesmerize his family with his prowess as a brilliant husband and remarkable father who knows all there is to know about instructing his wife and raising his kids. But Bob isn't going to let Leo enjoy a quiet summer by the lake."

I loved the book, *Baby Steps,* that Dr. Leo wrote in this movie and how Bob Wiley implemented baby steps to help him with his phobias and emotional issues.

When it comes to changing our long-standing habits and routines, it's often best to start with baby steps.

A lot of people fail with diets or getting in shape because they go hard-core for a short period of time and then stop all together because they can't maintain that pace.

When you haven't been prioritizing your well-being, it's important not to drastically change your life and your schedule all at one time.

A better plan is to make small, but consistent changes – baby steps.

Since you did the work to remove time-wasters from your life in the previous chapter, the next step is to add three acts of self-care to begin your day.

I have created a **Master Self Care list** in this chapter that will help you select those three acts of self-care. Because everyone is different and what works for one person might not work for someone else, I have given you lots of choices.

The #1 excuse people have for not taking care of their well-being is "I don't have the time."

In his book, *Miracle Morning,* author Hal Elrod says:

"Your level of success will rarely exceed your level of personal development, because success is something you attract by the person you become."

Elrod says most people are living a life of mediocrity and if you want a Level 10 life, then working on our personal development is the key:

> *"Our outer world will always be a reflection of our inner world. Our level of success is always going to parallel our level of personal development. Until we dedicate time each day to developing ourselves into the person we need to be to create the life we want, success is always going to be a struggle to attain."*

In *Make Your Bed* by Navy Seal Admiral William H. McRaven, he says "If you want to change the world, start off by making your bed."

How you begin your day matters.

Bestselling Author and blogger, Steve Pavlina, wrote this in a blog post:

> *"It's been said that the first hour is the rudder of the day. If I'm lazy or haphazard in my actions during the first hour after I wake up, I tend to have a fairly lazy and unfocused day. But if I strive to make that first hour optimally productive, the rest of the day tends to follow suit."*

I'm not a morning person. Never have been, never will be. I'm fortunate that I haven't had to set an alarm clock for years because I work for myself. In the early years of my self-employment, I wasted a lot of time because I had too much freedom. That's why I ended up developing my morning routine which has helped me in so many ways. I've been following this routine for years and make simple tweaks from time to time.

My morning routine looks like this:

- I make my bed
- I do a 20-minute mediation
- I write three pages in my personal journal
- I write five things I'm grateful for in my gratitude journal
- I read my Absolute No and Absolute Yes list
- I make a green smoothie (or other healthy breakfast)
- I do yoga (20-minute beginner back care yoga DVD by Rodney Yee) a few times a week
- I do some spiritual reading like: *A Course in Miracles*, Eckhart Tolle, Deepak Chopra, or many other inspiring books like *Women Who Run With the Wolves*, *The Artist Way*, or *This Time I Dance*
- I do a stretching routine for my neck, back and shoulders
- I do a short routine for my core on the exercise ball
- I lift weights one time per week with my personal trainer virtually
- I do a 3-mile walk (not always in the morning, but every day)
- I use essential oils
- I listen to relaxing music during this time

I have this daily checklist printed out and I use every day so I don't forget anything. When I do my morning routine, I feel great, and when I start skipping my routine for days, my life gets off balance quickly and not in a good way.

Below is a *Master Self-Care List* I put together. The goal is for you to choose three items that you will do every day as part of your new self-care routine. Of course, feel free to add anything to the list I have not included that makes you feel happy, fulfilled and joyful.

MASTER SELF-CARE LIST

- Meditation
- Make Your Bed
- Journal
- Gratitude List
- Read Your Absolute No and Your Absolute Yes List
- Drink A Healthy Smoothie
- Yoga
- Stretching
- Breathing
- Spiritual/Inspirational Reading
- Walking Outdoors
- Relaxation Music
- Prayer
- Hot Shower

- Warm Bath
- Skin Mask
- Facial
- Massage
- Sitting Outside in Nature
- Drinking Tea
- Essential Oils
- Affirmations
- Visualization
- Silence
- Exercise
- Reflection
- Self-Pleasure

Don't make time an excuse for not implementing a new morning routine.

Hal Elrod says you can having a morning routine in as little as six minutes when you are pressed for time. So, be flexible and don't think because you don't have 30 minutes or more in the morning, that you can't have your own Self-Care/Well-Being routine.

Start small. Consistency is what matters when you are beginning.

> Pick three items from the list above and create your own Morning Practice. Start your day with these three acts of self-care.

Find a quiet place in your home where you won't be disturbed and make your new practice sacred. You'll be amazed at how having this time to yourself to focus on your well-being can transform your entire day and life.

You are essentially saying "you matter" because now you are choosing to put your well-being first

At the end of this book is a resource section that you can use for some of these self-care action items on the Master List like the meditation app I use, spiritual books, and more.

Now, it's time to create your own soul-nourishing work and home environment.

CHAPTER 4: CREATING A SOUL-NOURISHING ENVIRONMENT

*"A sacred place is anywhere you can be
alone with your thoughts."*
~Susan Olsen

The most sacred place of all is the space within yourself. The place deep within your soul where you find peace and serenity; where you connect to your true and authentic self.

Having your morning self-care practice is the first step towards prioritizing your well-being. Your new morning practice will help you connect to your soul and the truth of who you are.

Now we are going to create a soul-nurturing physical environment.

As the saying goes, *"A messy room equals a messy mind."*

If we look around our homes, the clutter and disorganization are giving us a message.

In Feng Shui, which has been around for over four thousand years, the objective is to "assist individuals in creating environments that support and nurture their needs, desires and overall well-being."

Our environment does affect our energy; in Feng Shui they call this energy ch'i—the energy force that permeates all space around you.

In her book, *Feng Shui: Harmony by Design,* Nancy Santo Pietro says:

> **"Understanding and working with the principles of Feng Shui is the key to harnessing the power of chi' in a way that will support you and benefit your life and its various circumstances. The Feng Shui of your surroundings acts as a mirror image to your life and is interrelated..."**

I have read a lot of books on Feng Shui, and have applied these concepts to my home and I've always had great results.

On the website, www.fengshuiforreallife.com, author Carol Olmstead explains what our clutter means on a deeper level:

> "The Feng Shui definition for clutter is "postponed decisions and the inability to move forward." That means what you accumulate, where you put it, and why you keep it says a lot about you. We all have to deal with some amount of clutter, but according to Feng Shui principles, extreme clutter holds you back and keeps you from making progress.

> One of the basic tenets of Feng Shui is that nothing new flows into your life until you make room for it. Therefore, clearing clutter is the key to transforming your space. Feng Shui is about attracting harmony and abundance into your life, but clutter blocks good things from reaching you.

Clutter creates stagnation, encouraging a negative "putting-off-until-tomorrow" mentality rather than a positive "doing-it-today" focus, thereby reducing energy in our minds and in our spaces. Clutter in Feng Shui is defined as anything unfinished, unused, unresolved, or hopelessly disorganized. Since things that are loved and used have strong, active energy around them, when you surround yourself with your favorite things you add clarity and focus to your life. By contrast, when you surround yourself with things that you no longer love, or that hold negative memories, or are no longer useful, your life can lack direction.

Clutter represents stagnant energy, and it's one of the biggest issues that many of my Feng Shui clients face. It keeps you in the past, encourages procrastination, contributes to a lack of harmony in your home and makes you feel tired, overwhelmed, confused, angry, stuck, and depressed.

Studies show that of all the things we keep, we will only reuse one item in 20. That means that most people pile rather than file, cluttering their spaces with things they never use. Many people with clutter problems can't solve them because when they think of getting rid of things, they experience fear of loss. They are afraid that if they throw away items they have been saving they might never be able to replace them.

One way to avoid having to face the fear of getting rid of your clutter is to avoid accumulating all these things in the first place. Try turning any fears around: when you receive something — like a gift you don't really like or a memo you don't really need to save — ask yourself "how can I get rid of this" rather than "where can I keep it."

Where and why you have clutter says a lot about what is going on in your life. If you look at clutter all day, clutter is what you will attract into your life.

Here are some common clutter locations. What do they reveal about hidden aspects of your life?

- Clutter at the entrance of your home – may be concealing fear of relationships.

- Clutter in your closets – reveals an unwillingness to examine your emotions.

- Clutter in the kitchen – represents resentment of care-taking.

- Clutter next to your bed – symbolizes a desire for change or escape.

- Clutter under your bed - represents a fear of relationships.

- Clutter on a desk - reveals frustration, fear of letting go, and need to control.

- Clutter behind a door - means detachment from others.

- Clutter under furniture – represents concern with appearances.

- Clutter in a basement – reveals procrastination.

- Clutter in an attic – symbolizes living in the past.

- Clutter in a garage – reveals the inability to reach your potential.

- Clutter all over – reveals anger and low self-esteem."

I know for myself that when I take the time to de-clutter my home, I feel lighter, freer and more abundance and prosperity always flows into my life.

You don't have to be an expert or student of Feng Shui to know that our environment either supports us or it blocks us. A home that is disorganized, in disrepair, and disheveled is going to block our energy.

In his book, *From Stressy & Messy to Organized & Optimized*, author Bobby Jackson says the three biggest mistakes people make when it comes to getting organized are:

1. Organizing without decluttering first.

2. Repeatedly organizing the same space.

3. Procrastinating on organizing our space and consequently wasting time always looking for misplaced stuff.

According to studies, when your home is organized and optimized, you will have less anxiety and less stress on a physiological level. By taking the time to clean up your space, you will add more peace and serenity to your life as well as time.

In her New York Times bestselling book, *The Life-Changing Magic of Tidying Up,* author Marie Kondo says:

"When you put your house in order, you put your affairs and your past in order, too."

So why do most people fail at putting their house in order?

Marie Kondo says because people do a little at a time and don't see visible results or feel the effects. Also because they take the easy route and leap at "storage methods" that promise quick and convenient ways to remove visible clutter. She doesn't advise the storage method.

Her method is NOT a baby steps method, but more of a MARATHON METHOD.

She suggests that tidying up must always start with discarding.

Marie says there are three types of people who can't stay tidy:

1. Can't throw it away type

2. Can't put it back type

3. A combination of 1 and 2

In her course, she begins with these words of wisdom:

"Tidying is a special event. Don't do it every day."

Of course, we clean up our dishes, do our laundry, vacuum, and do our chores. What Marie is talking about is a special event of putting your house in order.

If your house does not bring you peace and serenity, then take the following Marie Kondo steps:

1. Visualize your space and how you want it to be.

2. Focus on what you want to keep; not what you want to discard.

3. Go through this process by taking each item in your hands and asking, "Does this spark joy?" If it does, keep it. If it does not, dispose of it. The key is to touch each item.

4. Do one category at a time instead of one room at a time. The categories are:
    a. Clothing
        i. Tops
        ii. Bottoms
        iii. Socks
        iv. Undergarments
        v. Pajamas
        vi. Bags
        vii. Accessories
        viii. Swimsuits
        ix. Work Clothing
        x. Shoes
    b. Kitchenware
    c. Décor
    d. Books
    e. Papers
    f. Mementos (always do this last as it is the hardest)

5. When you have discarded items that don't bring you joy, you will either donate or throw them away. Some people may take them to a consignment shop. The key is to remove them from your house. Once you've done this, then it's time to organize what you are keeping.

6. When it comes to your clothing, fold them so you have easy access to them and it solves your storage problems. Marie recommends storying things standing up rather than laying them flat. Also, in your closet arrange heavy items to the left side and lighter items to the right. As you move towards the right side of the closet, the length of the clothing grows shorter, the material thinner and the color lighter.

Clearing your space is the art of letting go.

When we can't let go of things it's usually due to one of two reasons:

1. Attachment to the past

2. Fear of the future

I find it fascinating how much our "stuff" reveals about us.

Last year I attended a 3-day emotional healing retreat. This had nothing to do with clearing decluttering. It was body work regarding deep emotional clearing.

However, when I returned home from this retreat, I felt the need to go through everything in my house and get rid of stuff. It's like I was purging my past.

On the first day of purging, I packed 12 green lawn bags full of clothing and shoes. For more than a week, I went through every closet and every area of my house and packed stuff up to discard or donate. I threw away a lot of junk and also had a nonprofit company come to my home and pick up what could be donated to others.

I felt amazing after doing this thorough decluttering; as a result, my business tripled last year. I attribute this to all the emotional healing work I did.

When we clean up one area of our lives, it usually has a domino effect and will cause us to clean up other areas of our lives.

In my book, *Stop Living Paycheck-to-Paycheck*, I share how I saved $100k in 12 months. This also happened after I attended the emotional healing workshop. Once I got home, I realized I was making a lot of money, but not saving a lot and decided it was important for my financial well-being to make saving money my #1 priority.

My business grew and my savings grew; within one year, I had saved $100k. That means if an emergency came up, I could live comfortably for two years without working. I can't believe how doing the emotional healing work caused me to clean up relationships, set boundaries, save money and declutter my home.

In the resource section at the end of this book, I'll share with you the information about that 3-day retreat that changed my life.

If you've been neglecting yourself for a long time, as many women do who have a ton of responsibilities, do not feel bad. You have a good heart, you are conscientious, you are a loving, giving person.

I hope you are seeing that if you don't take care of yourself first, you can't fulfill your dreams, achieve your goals or take care of others in a healthy way; and by investing your time in creating a soul-nourishing environment, you are taking care of yourself.

I wouldn't say my home is picture perfect or up to Marie Kondo's standards, but for now, I feel it is organized, optimized and makes me feel peaceful and serene.

Give yourself the gift of creating a soul-nourishing environment – it is part of your self-care.

If the Marie Kondo *Marathon Method* works for you, then start there. If not, start by naming your clutter areas and one by one, clear them up.

Your life will improve in so many ways when you do this.

Next up is the 10 Laws of Setting Boundaries that most over-givers struggle with…

CHAPTER 5: 10 LAWS OF BOUNDARIES FOR WOMEN WHO GIVE TOO MUCH

Recently, new neighbors moved in to the house across the street. They started doing a lot of home remodeling, built a pier, brought a large boat, and there were several cars and people coming and going in that house.

About two months later, I noticed the neighbor in the adjacent house put up a fence separating her property from the new owners' property. I found it interesting since she has been in her house for 20+ years, and so had the previous owners of the neighboring house.

Something made her decide to draw a line and separate her property from the new owners. By the way, she only put up the new fence on that one side. The other side had a natural separation with hedges.

Dr. Henry Cloud and Dr. John Townsend, authors of *Boundaries*, say this:

> *"Any confusion of responsibility and ownership in our lives is a problem of boundaries. Just as homeowners set physical property lines around their land, we need to set mental, physical, emotional and spiritual boundaries for our lives to help us distinguish what is our responsibility and what isn't."*

As women, we are raised to take care of others and to get our esteem from what we do for others, making it easy to start taking on the responsibility of others in the name of being a good girl.

The problem with taking on other's responsibilities, however, is after a while, we end up drained, exhausted, and often resentful because the other person either expects this treatment, feels entitled and/or doesn't appreciate it.

So, whose problem is it? Ours or theirs?

Drs. Cloud and Townsend answer this question:

"It is easy to misunderstand boundaries. At first glance, it seems as if the individual who has difficulty setting limits is the one who has the boundary problem; however, people who don't respect others' limits also have boundary problems."

So the answer is that both parties are at fault. Since you can't control other people, you will work on what you can control: yourself.

In the physical world, boundaries are easy to see – fences, signs, walls, hedges, etc., but in the relationship world, they often get blurred.

By knowing what is our responsibility, we have more freedom. We are not responsible for other people, except for our children, of course.

When we try to "rescue" others from the natural consequences of their behavior, we render them powerless.

When we are able to set limits with warmth and consequences, then we produce confidence in others giving them a sense of control in their own lives.

Boundary setting has not come easy for me. I've had to work with therapists and healers to learn to set boundaries with others. It was a process, not a one-and-done event. Eventually I got better and better at setting boundaries in my personal life as well as in my business.

Self-care is about learning to set boundaries in your relationships, and that's why I've dedicated an entire chapter in this book to it.

When you set boundaries with others, not only will it free up more of your time since you won't be doing tasks that are not your responsibility, but it will allow you to replenish yourself physically, emotionally and spiritually by setting limits.

Based on the book, *Boundaries*, which sold over 2 million copies, let's take a look at the 10 Laws of Boundaries:

Law #1 – The Law of Sowing and Reaping which is the law of cause and effect. Boundaries force the person who is doing the work (the sowing) to also receive the benefit (reaping).

Law #2 – The Law of Responsibility says that problems arise when boundaries of responsibility are confused.

Law #3 – The Law of Power says that you will have more power when you set limits and boundaries.

Law #4 - The Law of Respect says we need to love the boundaries of others in order to command respect for our own.

Law #5 – The Law of Motivation says that giving is not love when we give to others out of a fear of losing love.

Law #6 – The Law of Evaluation says we need to examine the pain our setting limits and boundaries with others causes and see how this hurt is helpful to others and sometimes the it is the best thing we can do for them and the relationship.

Law #7 – The Law of Proactivity says proactive boundaries are better than reactive boundaries.

Law #8 – The Law of Envy says that envy is a self-perpetuating cycle because it shows us where we are lacking.

Law #9 – The Law of Activity says that passivity never pays off. We have to work and push ourselves in life.

Law #10 – The Law of Exposure says that your boundaries need to be made visible to others and communicated to them in the relationship.

Make a list of people or situations whom you need to set boundaries.

It's important to know that there are four types of people that will NOT respect your limits and boundary setting:

1. **Compliant** – Compliant people are chameleons. Their inability to say no to the bad is pervasive. They were

usually raised to never say no. Essentially, they say yes to the bad.

2. **Avoidant** – Avoidant people say no to the good; they have an inability to ask for help, to recognize one's own needs and to let others in.

3. **Controllers** – These people do not respect other people's boundaries and think *maybe* means *yes*. Sometimes, controllers can be aggressive which manifests as being verbally and/or physically abusive. They are unaware that other people have boundaries and think that everyone should say *yes* to whatever they ask. Manipulative controllers are those people who try to persuade people not to set boundaries with them so they can get their way. It's all about their needs, and it is often at the expense of other people.

4. **Non-Responsive** – These people simply don't hear the needs of others. The don't allow for other's feelings, wants or needs. They don't care.

Do you have any people in your life who fit into these categories?

One of my ex-boyfriends was an avoidant and could not let anything good into his life. He was also a controller and did not respect when I told him *no*. To him, it was a game to turn my *no* into a *yes*.

Look at the list of people that you need to set boundaries with and, if applicable, next to their name, write down if they fit into one of these additional categories.

People who become angry with you for setting boundaries are self-centered and see others as extensions of themselves. Angry people have a character problem. But, guess what? That's not your problem.

These people may get angry at you when you set boundaries and they may try to make you feel guilty. They may act hurt or disappointed. That's okay. Let them do what they do and decide for yourself what is right for you.

I avoided setting boundaries in some of my intimate relationships because of my fear of abandonment. Many times, when I set boundaries, the relationship ended because it was not based on mutual respect or a mutual give-and-take that a healthy relationship should have. Instead, it was me over-giving to the other person because I mistakenly believed if I did *enough*, he would stay. When I set boundaries, stopped over-giving, then the other person wasn't happy. That's okay. It's very freeing to speak your truth, stop over-giving, state your needs and to have clear boundaries in place. And to also not be controlled by a fear of abandonment.

When you look at your list of people you need to set boundaries with, who are you afraid of disappointing?

When it is a close family member, it makes it harder. Sometimes we just try to keep the peace in the family and this allows people to walk all over us.

As we begin to set boundaries with others, there will be a loss because the person we set boundaries with probably will experience a "hole" in their lives. The hole represents what you were doing for them – maybe you were paying their bills, maybe you were cleaning up after them, maybe you were spending a lot of time with them. When you remove the "over-giving" from their lives, they will feel an emptiness. They will probably feel hurt and disappointed.

It's time for you to give yourself permission to disappoint others.

This does not mean you shouldn't set boundaries with them. The *emptiness* or *hole* they feel as a result of you setting boundaries is the work they need to do on themselves. It is not your responsibility to fix them or fill the hole.

> Who is the number one BOUNDARY-BUSTER in your life right now? Make a list of how you will begin setting boundaries with this person.

I've found for me that it helps to set one or two boundaries at a time if there are numerous boundary issues with one person.

Disappointment is bound to happen. We all will disappoint others and there is no way we can get through this life without doing so. Don't let that deter you from setting boundaries.

Self-care is about setting good boundaries and protecting yourself.

Recently, I needed to set a boundary with one of my clients on a book project we were working on. I had procrastinated for weeks about doing it and it was getting out of hand. A therapist and intuitive I was working with helped me create the sandwich method of setting boundaries.

We started out with one positive about the person or project, then added the boundary, and ended with another positive. POSITIVE/NEGATIVE/POSITIVE.

She helped me write out what to say without coming across as overly angry or resentful. **Here's how it went:**

1. Great book, great message, great project.

2. Boundaries – Scope of the project had doubled, and this is what needs to happen now.

3. Let's get this book done and out into the world in a timely manner. We can do it.

Surprisingly, my client agreed to all the boundaries that I set in the email. I was shocked, and the rest of the project went smoothly and with ease.

When I look back on this, I think it's funny how I avoided setting boundaries even though I knew it was what had to be done to protect myself, my time and my business.

Who are you procrastinating about setting boundaries with? Why are your procrastinating?

Questions That Arise on Setting Boundaries

1. What if I hurt the other person's feelings?

2. Am I being selfish?

3. Why do I feel guilty when I set boundaries with others?

4. Shouldn't I be giving unconditional love to others?

5. Can I set limits and still be a loving person?

Misguided Reasons We Don't Set Boundaries

- Fear of not being seen as spiritual
- Fear of punishment
- Fear of love or attention being withdrawn
- Fear of abandonment
- Fear of hurting the other person's feelings
- Fear of anger from the other person
- A hidden wish to be totally dependent on another
- Fear of being seen as bad or selfish

We are not meant to be doormats to others. It is not selfish to make others take responsibility in their lives.

Loving others is allowing them to take responsibility for their own life. When we set limits, it benefits us and the other person.

Of course, we do get "push back" when we set limits with other people who are accustomed to us NOT setting limits with them.

I broke up with a man I had been seeing for four years and he didn't understand why I wanted things to change. He wanted things to stay the same and he tried to make me feel guilty for wanting more in the relationship.

I ended our relationship and eventually had to block him because I didn't want the negative energy in my life. He didn't accept my boundaries.

Sometimes we have to be harsh with our boundaries if others are not respecting them.

Everyone in my life told me for a long time that I should block this man, but it wasn't until I saw how much time and energy he was sucking out of my life that I finally did it.

Just like a leech sucks blood and thrives on that, so do boundary-blockers and boundary-less people. They suck our time, energy, and our dreams. It's in our best interest to set limits with these people even if they are relatives, clients, friends and people we deeply care about.

> Now that you've written your list of people you need to set boundaries with, begin this week by setting one "easy" boundary and work up to the harder ones.

If you need help with this, I recommend working with a good therapist who can help you start setting boundaries.

I've found that often people who are not good at setting boundaries with others did not have their boundaries respected when they were children.

Don't let your past ruin your future. Adults set boundaries. You are no longer a powerless child. You have the power to set boundaries with everyone in your life, and when you do so, you will take back your power.

Next, we are going to talk about the disease to please…

CHAPTER 6: OVERCOMING THE DISEASE TO PLEASE

Let me ask you some questions…

- Do you hate disappointing others?
- Do you try to never let other people down (even if their demands are excessive or unreasonable)?
- Do you feel guilty when you say NO to others?
- Do you always try to please others even at the expense of your own feelings?
- Is it important to you that everyone in your life like you?
- Do you avoid conflict and confrontation?
- Do you feel guilty when you say NO to others?
- Do you put the needs of people you love ahead of your own?

If you answered "Yes" to any of these questions, you have what psychologist and bestselling author, Harriet B. Braiker, Ph.D, calls *the disease to please.*

In her book, *The Disease to Please,* Braiker says, "The disease to please is a compulsive—even addictive behavior pattern. As a people pleaser, you feel controlled by your need to please others and addicted to their approval."

THE PRICE OF NICE

Being nice is a cover-up for a deep fear of negative emotions.

I am a recovering people pleaser, so I know first-hand about the disease to please. It derives from having an image of niceness instead of being real, and showing anger, displeasure, or disappointment when necessary.

Dr. Braiker says, "Niceness is the psychological armor of the people pleaser."

Basically, it's a defense mechanism that we use. It's how we try to protect ourselves and something that probably developed in childhood. Here's what she says:

"The belief in the protective power of niceness, then, is holdover from a childhood era of magical thinking. Fears of rejection, abandonment, isolation or disapproval – and of the depression and emotional pain such experiences can produce – are now the "monsters" that require containment. But, the dread of rejection, alienation, and loneliness are reality-based fears, not fantasy -based fears, like the imaginary inhabitants of a child's closet."

Niceness was something we most likely developed to protect ourselves as children, but as adults, this does not work. It's not realistic to be nice all the time and not be able to express negative emotions.

Being nice doesn't protect you from verbal or emotional abuse by others. It doesn't protect you from people who are being unkind. As adults, we do not want to reward people with our niceness and pretend everything is okay when they treat us badly.

Being nice all the time is very stressful and difficult to maintain.

As people pleasers, we have a number of unwritten "Shoulds" that we follow, like:

- We should always do what others want, expect or need from us.
- We should take care of everyone around us whether they ask for help or not.
- We should always listen to everyone's problems and try to solve them.
- We should always be nice and never disappoint anyone or hurt their feelings.
- We should never say no to anyone who needs or requests something of us.
- We should always be happy and upbeat and never show negative feelings to others.
- We should never burden people with our own needs and problems.

People pleasers care more about others than themselves. We are also pros at giving, but not receiving.

Another manifestation of being a people pleaser is being a perfectionist.

Of course, there is nothing wrong with having high standards; but striving for perfection is demoralizing and a recipe for failure. Instead, we should strive for excellence.

IT'S OKAY NOT TO BE NICE

This should be added to your list of daily affirmations – it's okay not to be nice.

People with the disease to please have distorted thinking and feel selfish when it comes to taking care of themselves. I know I did. The two choices seem to be:

1. Be selfless; always putting other people's needs ahead of yours;

2. Be completely selfish, always putting your needs first and foremost;

This is black-and-white thinking, and people pleasers are missing a third choice.

Dr. Braiker calls it "enlightened self-interest" which means that you take good care of yourself, even putting your needs first at times, while simultaneously considering the needs of others.

It will take practice to do this. For people pleasers, the volume is turned down on their own needs and on high towards the needs of others.

We have to learn to say NO to others.

"Without the ability to say 'NO' or to effectively delegate, prioritize, negotiate, or ask for help, the stream of continuous demands from others goes unfiltered and unregulated."

You can care about others and look after yourself. There is a big difference between being too selfish and having enlightened self-interest.

It is not always better to give than to receive. The best balance in relationships is for both parties to give and receive.

> I want you to create flashcards to remind you that you are moving towards becoming a recovered people-pleaser. Write the following statements on the cards.

- It is okay to say NO
- I can take a time out
- I can delegate
- It's okay not to be nice
- Self-Respect is setting limits with others
- I speak up for myself
- No "Shoulds"
- Sandwich technique
- Self-Approval
- Self-Preservation
- Recovering in small steps

- I take care of me
- I set boundaries with others
- I have the courage to change
- I love myself
- I respect myself
- No guilt
- I matter
- Negative emotions are okay
- I give myself permission to disappoint others

Include reading these flash cards in your morning routine to remind you of the work you are doing on yourself.

In the next chapter, we are going to talk about *not* saying Yes when you want to say No.

CHAPTER 7: DON'T SAY YES WHEN YOU WANT TO SAY NO

Think of saying no as a new skill you need to learn. As someone who has been an over-giver, people pleaser, and nice girl – you probably say yes more than you say no.

Yes is a default response to people pleasers and a bad habit.

Break this habit in five steps:

1. Step 1: Delay giving an immediate response when someone makes a request of you

2. Step 2: Identify your options in the next 24-48 hours

3. Step 3: Think about the consequences of your options

4. Step 4: Select the best option for you

5. Step 5: Respond to the request/invitation/demand firmly and directly with one of the following options:

    a. Say NO

    b. Offer a counter-proposal

    c. Say YES

By giving yourself time and not automatically saying yes to every request, you will begin saying no more often.

You've heard the saying, "Think before you speak." That's the basis of this new skill. Create time between an invitation, demand, and request. As you do this, your sense of control will increase and so will your sense of confidence.

Will others be disappointed when we tell them no? Absolutely, and that's okay.

We are learning to do what's right for us and not what's right for everyone else.

Saying "Yes" is usually a knee-jerk response that people pleasers have. Taking a time-out and not responding right away, we are doing what I call a "Pattern-Interrupt."

Here are some PHRASES TO BUY TIME you can use when others make requests of you:

- I'll need to check my schedule and get back to you.
- I might have a conflict. I'll check this out and get back to you with an answer as soon as I can.
- I'm unable to give you an answer right at this moment. I'll get back to you on that.
- I'm not sure I'll have the time to do that, I'll let you know tomorrow/next few days/next week.
- I need some time to think about that. I'll let you know shortly.

We need practice using these new responses. It has become second nature to say yes to requests of our time.

Because I was a paralegal for 17 years, I constantly get requests from friends and family members to help them with their legal issues. In the past, I always said yes to every request.

Now, I implement the 24-hour rule and give myself time to respond. Instead of saying yes to every request, I've learned instead to provide resources like attorneys I can refer them to or other avenues for them to get help. This has saved a lot of my time.

Here's the thing – I love the law and I love helping people with legal issues. However, I'm not an attorney and don't have a license to practice law. So, as much as I'd love to help everyone, I acknowledge my limits. Now I'm able to refer people to others who can help them with their legal issues in a professional manner.

> What area of your life or who in your life do you always say YES to?

In addition to legal questions, I find people are always asking me to help create or update their resume'. I previously had a resume' writing service, and a lot of people know this. Now that I charge money to do resumes, people don't ask me as much. I give people a sample resume so they can create their own resume themselves.

> Think of alternative ways you can say NO and perhaps give others some options or helpful resources.

To make sure you start implementing the 24-hour rule (or 48 hours or 72 hours or whatever works for you), write the PHRASES TO BUY TIME on index cards or post-it notes and put them on your desk, in your purse, near your phone, and anywhere you need a visual reminder *not* to say YES and to give yourself time to respond.

Learning to say NO will give you more time for your own self-care.

Next up is learning to ask for help and delegating, which is another time-giver…

CHAPTER 8: TAG, YOU'RE IT! LEARNING TO ASK FOR HELP

Having raised three kids as a single mom while working full time as a paralegal, I had to learn the art and skill of delegating.

By the time my kids were 12, they knew how to do laundry, make some easy dinners, take care of the dog, clean their rooms (dust, vacuum, put things away) and help around the house.

When they were younger, I had a bad habit of doing everything for them. That was not teaching them anything and was enabling them to leave their toys and clothes on the floor and not take care of themselves.

When we do things for others that they can do for themselves, we take away their ability to be self-sufficient.

It does feel good to "give," but this book is about over-giving and that's why you're reading it. Of course, as women, we love to be nurturers and to take care of others – but we cannot continue to do so at the expense of ourselves.

There are only so many hours in the day. And in the 24/7 technology, modern world we live in, we simply can't do it all. We have to learn to let go of the reins and start delegating – in our personal lives, at work and in our business.

Years ago, I was working with my amazing business coach, Jason Nyback, and I was becoming burnt out and exhausted from all the clients I was getting in my done-for-you bestselling author program. Consequently, I scheduled an emergency call with my coach and told him how I was feeling. He suggested I do three things:

1. Start charging more

2. Start doing less

3. Hire others and start delegating

I took his advice and did all three. I looked at my packages and removed some of the done-for-you services; I increased my prices and hired some new assistants in my business.

This solved my problem. If I had not done those three things, I might not be in business today because I was seriously burnt out at the time.

Burn out happens when we do too much for others and don't delegate.

With anything new, there is a transition period. In my business, I had to make a list of what tasks could be delegated to others. Then, I had to hire the right people who could perform those tasks, and I had to train them.

I avoided delegating because I didn't want to invest the time in hiring and training others. However, that investment has paid off over and over. I can focus on my core competencies and not get burnt-out and over-burdened with all the details of running my business.

I think about companies who are masters at delegating, like Amazon, and I imagine if Jeff Bezos had a mindset of doing everything himself; he'd be out of business.

Another reason I did everything myself in my business was because I misguidedly thought, "No one can do this better than me." Boy, was I wrong. I have assistants that do a lot of things better than me.

Of course, if you're a perfectionist and think there is only one way to do something, then you might struggle with delegating. Just try to strive for *good enough* instead of *perfection* as you start learning the art of delegating.

Whether you are delegating in business, work or at home – people may balk when you start to assign responsibilities to them. That's okay. Don't accept helplessness as an excuse. Even small children can help with daily chores.

My 2 ½ year old granddaughter knows how to clean up her toys and organize them in bins. My daughter plays the "clean up" song on YouTube and my granddaughter sings it while cleaning up her toys.

3 Steps to Get Started Delegating

1. Identify the tasks that need to be delegated and the people to whom you will delegate those tasks.

2. Write a script for effective delegation

3. Practice your script and eliminate all apologies or guilt or discomfort language.

If you are not accustomed to delegating, then having a written script that you rehearse will help you get comfortable with this new skill.

Here's a sample script:

You: Hi honey. I need you to do the laundry. Let me show you how the machines work and how much detergent to use. If you have any questions, let me know.

Son: What? Why do I have to do the laundry? You always do the laundry.

You: I understand that I've always done your laundry in the past. However, you're older now and it's time for you to learn how to do it yourself. I know this is new for you, but you'll get the hang of it pretty quickly. When your laundry is dried, let me know and I'll show you how to fold it and put it away.

Son: But I have plans with my friends.

You: Let your friends know that you have some chores to do and you'll meet them as soon as you're done.

Son: Okay mom.

The conversation may not go exactly like this. You might get a lot of push back, or none at all. The point is to have it written down, to not take on any guilt and to be effective in your delegating – direct, brief and to the point.

Do not apologize for delegating. You need others to accept responsibility for their lives, and they need to learn new skills to be self-sufficient. The younger, the better.

If you need to delegate at work or in your business, then you also want to have a script. Be aware that there will be a transition period in which you will identify the tasks that need to be delegated, train the other person, and let go of the reins.

In my business, any time I decide to delegate a task, I create a Standard Operating Procedure (SOP). I write down all the steps needed for that task and I usually include a training video. Once my assistant goes through the training, then the first time they do the task, we do it together. If I feel confident, they can do it on their own, then I allow them to take over that task from me.

Again, if I had not learned to delegate in my business, I probably would not have a business.

Some books that helped me learn this skill are:

- *The E-Myth* by Michael Gerber
- *Work the System* by Sam Carpenter
- *Clockwork* by Mike Michalowicz

In the book *Work the System,* the author says, "Dysfunction is gold!" That's because inefficiency teaches us how to eliminate it and correct it. When we fix the dysfunction, we find our gold!

Think about this:

"How do you describe your typical day? Is it an amorphous, complex jumble of happenings or is it relaxed and ordered sequence of events? Is it chaotic or is it under control? Do you have enough money? Do you spend time with family and friends? Through the day – and through your life – are you in an endless race around a circular track or are you climbing slowly and steadily toward a mountaintop? Are you getting what you want? If not, could it be a personal management problem?"

If we thought of our lives as a business, we would see if things are out of control then we have a personal management problem.

You must have more control over the details of your life if you want to have more peace and success.

Sam Carpenter says:

"The lure of dancing in the meadow is an invitation to illusionary bliss. Truth is, orderliness and attention to detail are the roots of peace. Proof? Consider the indisputable reverse logic: in any setting, the opposite of peace – disorder – always leading to desperation."

We don't want to make desperate decisions. If we invest the time in identifying where our lives are *inefficient* and not working, then look at the details and fix the dysfunction, we will make decisions from a higher and more grounded place.

We fix dysfunction by:

- Learning to say no
- Learning to delegate
- Learning to prioritize our well-being
- Learning it's okay not to be nice
- Learning it's okay to disappoint others
- Learning to set boundaries and limits with others
- Learning to remove things that aren't working in our lives
- Learning self-care

If you want more order in your life, practice these skills. Once you learn to ask for help, you will feel empowered. Think of all the people that ask you for help. It has to be a two-way street; you can't only be the one offering help. Maybe it's time for you to be the one asking for help.

If you are a strong independent woman, you have learned through trial and error that you cannot continue to do everything for everyone. Asking for help is a sign of maturity and wisdom. It's how we evolve and how businesses evolve. It is a sign of strength and freedom.

Next up, is learning the skill of protecting our energy from toxic people we may encounter in our lives…

CHAPTER 9: PROTECTING YOUR ENERGY FROM TOXIC PEOPLE

On one of my calls with my therapist and spiritual advisor, she said, "Michelle, you are an empath and you take on the energy of those around you. Right now, the reason you are feeling so depleted is because you are taking on the toxic energy of everyone around you."

So, she had me do a meditation where I envisioned myself in a clear bubble that protected me from other people's energy. On the outside of the bubble was a pyramid with mirrors on it to deflect negative energy. She suggested I do this protective energy meditation daily.

If you live with other people, it's important that you don't take on their negative energy.

I find that being a recovering people pleaser, I pick up the negative energy of people around me very easily. As a child, I thought the problems other people had were somehow my fault. As an adult, we have to allow people to take responsibility for their energy, their moods and their life. It's no longer our responsibility.

Just now, my daughter came in my room and said, "I thought you were going to the store." She said it with a major attitude, and then I started going into guilt mode because I did say I would go to the store in the morning. However, I needed to finish the last two chapters of this book, so I made a decision to do that first.

I started to feel guilty about this decision. Then, I took a time-out to do my protective energy meditation and to check in with myself. This reflection time reminded me to be careful what I say to others and to keep my word. It also reminded me that I also have priorities and commitments, like writing a book a month, and it's okay if I decide to make a change in my schedule. Going to the grocery store wasn't a life and death issue.

Do you see how the lines can get blurred when people have expectations of us?

We must be very aware of what we promise or say to others because they will hold us to it.

That's why having the 24-hour rule when it comes to requests of our time is paramount. I still am working on this because I sometimes say things I don't always mean just to pacify the other person. Then, I change my mind and feel like I disappointed them.

Remember, there is a lesson in everything. As soon as you start doing this work and becoming more aware, you will have lots of learning situations come up like the one I just had.

What have I learned:

- Be impeccable with my word
- Don't promise things I can't deliver
- Set my priorities and don't over commit
- Don't say YES when I want to say NO

- Don't take on unhealthy guilt; just observe and make changes as necessary

We are not perfect. We are all flaw-some!

This was a good learning experience for me.

We don't want to take on the toxic energy of others, but sometimes we can learn from the toxic energy.

My daughter had an *attitude* because I made a promise and didn't keep it. That's okay. I'm learning.

Now, what if you have people in your life who are selfish to the point of being a narcissist, psychopath or sociopath?

In her book, *Women Who Love Psychopaths*, author Sandra L. Brown, M.A., says:

"Intimacy is a byproduct of a healthy relationship... Dysfunctional or inadequate intimacy means the very thing a survivor is striving for in a relationship cannot be attained, as the disorder prevents deep connection, and the duration of intimacy itself is likely to be short-lived despite the length of the relationship... the disordered person doesn't even desire true closeness."

She goes on to describe the four skills needed in a healthy relationship:

1. Self-Identity
2. Self-Direction
3. Empathy
4. Intimacy

Without these, other people will be harmed by the disordered person.

Have you ever found yourself in a dysfunctional relationship and asked the question, "Why is this person like this?" Or "What is wrong with this person?"

As Sandra Brown likes to say, *"They are sicker than we are smart?"*

If someone truly has a mental illness such as narcissism, borderline personality disorder, psychopath, sociopath, etc., you are never going to understand *why* they do what they do.

They have a mental disorder that will never make sense to you or satisfy your logical brain.

When they say it takes two to tango, they are right in that disordered people need victims and they typically seek out partners with what Sandra Brown calls "Super-Traits":

1. Highly conscientious people

2. Self-Disciplined

3. Responsible

4. Organized

5. Dependable

6. Resourceful

7. Purposeful

8. High desire to work things out

If you are in a relationship with a disordered person, you are probably frustrated, angry, exhausted and traumatized.

Sandra Brown says that 90% of victims have some form of trauma-like symptoms and 50-75% of them have full blown PTSD.

She recommends that you get treated for the trauma you have. Being in a relationship with someone with a mental disorder is traumatizing and you probably need professional help.

I would recommend visiting Sandra Brown's website at: SafeRelationshipsMagazine.com.

She also has an affordable online program (which I have taken and it's amazing): SafeRelationshipsMagazine.com/Living-Recovery-Program-4

Recovering from disordered people is something we need help doing.

Since going through Sandra's program, I have been able to remove a toxic relationship with an ex and implement the no-contact rule.

A good rule of thumb is if you feel stressed out, confused, drained and bad about yourself after you have contact with this person, then it's important to minimize your time with them, get professional help and remove all contact with them if possible.

If you're reading this book, you most likely have many of those *Super-Traits* and you are being sought out by disordered people; so it would not surprise me if you are currently in or have been in a relationship with a disordered person.

Another book I recommend all women read is *The Gift of Fear* by Gavin DeBecker.

I didn't realize how naïve I was until I read his book. As women, we are often the prey of dangerous people, and we need to protect ourselves.

The author says:

"Americans are experts at denial… Denial is a save-now-pay-later scheme, a contract written entirely in small print, for in the long run, the denying person knows the truth on some level, and it causes a constant low-grade anxiety."

Who in your life is causing you anxiety? Make a list right now.

When another person causes us anxiety, it could be because we haven't set boundaries with them, or we are taking care of their responsibilities or because we are over-giving. It can also be because they are a disordered person and they need professional help.

Unfortunately, as Sandra Brown talks about in her book, because of their brain chemistry, these disordered people rarely change. So, if you are in a relationship and are hoping the other person will change, you are probably wasting your time.

One concept in *The Gift of Fear* that opened my eyes is that millions of people have a belief that people are infinitely good and, therefore, we ignore signals and become victims.

These signals are red flags and your internal warning system is telling you something is amiss. If you believe all people have good intentions, then you will deny the signals and red flags.

The author goes on to say:

"We, in contrast to every other creature in nature, choose not to explore – and even to ignore – survival signals. The mental energy we use searching for the innocent explanation to everything could more constructively be applied to evaluating the environment for important information."

What red flags and signals are you ignoring right now with someone in your life?

These are the blinders we all wear.

A good exercise is to write down all the negatives and red flags about that person and then pretend you are trying to set up this person with a family member or your best friend. Write it out how that conversation would go.

Here's an example:

"I have this guy I wanted you to meet. He is unemotionally available. He only cares about himself and doesn't care about what you need. He will disappear for days after you've shared an intimate evening together. He won't send your flowers or tell you how he feels or spend much time with you. He will waste your time on the phone talking all about himself. He is also good at turning arguments against you and making them be all your fault; he never takes responsibility for his actions. Would you like to go out with him?"

I once did this exercise with a guy I was dating and it was a wakeup call. I would never want this guy to date someone I cared about. Do this exercise like you are recommending this person to someone you care about. It will open your eyes.

Sometimes we keep toxic people in our lives because we are addicted to drama. When we don't have the drama, our lives may feel empty, lonely and void.

That's okay. When you remove anything – including toxic people, time-wasters, boundary-busters, energy vampires – there will always be a void.

And that leads us to the next chapter, which is all about adding self-care to your schedule so you can fill up the void with healthy acts.

You deserve to have a happy, joyful, and drama-free life!

CHAPTER 10: PRIORITZING SELF-CARE IN TO YOUR SCHEDULE

Congratulations! You have come a long way. So much of creating a life you love is about removing what is not working and what is sucking your time and energy.

In Chapter 3, I laid out the **Master Self-Care list**, which you'll find again below.

Once you have established your daily morning routine with at least three items from your self-care list, and you've done that for at least 30 days, then you can begin adding more self-care acts into your schedule.

Circle 5-10 items on the Master Self-Care List that speak to you and schedule them into your calendar now.

MASTER SELF-CARE LIST

- Meditation
- Make your Bed
- Journal
- Gratitude List
- Read Your Absolute No and Your Absolute Yes list
- Drink a Healthy Smoothie
- Yoga

- Stretching
- Breathing
- Spiritual/Inspirational Reading
- Walking Outdoors
- Relaxation Music
- Prayer
- Hot Shower
- Warm Bath
- Skin Mask
- Facial
- Massage
- Sitting Outside In Nature
- Drinking Tea
- Essential Oils
- Affirmations
- Visualization
- Silence
- Exercise
- Reflection
- Self-Pleasure

Another suggestion I have is to automate some of these items. For example, I pay for a monthly recurring massage and schedule these in advance. Additionally, I walk every day at the same time. I make my bed as soon as I get out of bed. And of course, my daily routine keeps things on automatic pilot so I don't have to think about them.

The goal is to "not" have to think about these things and to create a routine and ritual for yourself. Automate or schedule as many things as you can.

People in your life may become uncomfortable when they see you taking care of yourself, and they may even call you selfish. That's okay. You know deep down that if you don't take care of your well-being, you cannot continue to care for those you love.

My routines have saved my life. They set the tone for my entire day and they also give my life structure.

You deserve to enjoy your life and to take time for self-care!

CLOSING THOUGHTS

As I was working on this book, I went back and forth on what the subtitle should be. I conducted some surveys and chose the subtitle. Then, in the middle of the night (which is when spirit often wakes me up with book titles and creative ideas), I knew I needed to change one word in the subtitle.

I emailed the cover designer and asked her to make the change. I felt good about it. By the next morning, I was questioning this decision.

Coincidentally, I had an appointment with my therapist and spiritual healer, Nanci Deutsch. I told her about how I was conflicted and she asked, "What changed from yesterday when you felt confident and self-assured about the subtitle to today?"

The answer was, instead of going within, I started getting into my head. Then, I texted several people asking which subtitle they liked, and of course, received conflicting answers.

She asked me if any of those people I texted were intuitive or spiritual people that would lead with their guidance and intuition rather than their ego and intellect. I said no.

She then suggested that I begin to create a sacred circle of people in my life that were more spiritually aligned, intuitive and on the path of personal growth and healing.

Think about the five people you spend the most time with or talk to most often. Where are they in their lives? If we are going to change and start putting ourselves first, it's important we bring people into our life that are doing the same.

Begin now to create your own Sacred Circle of people who are on the same path or ahead of you on the path.

I recently had a call with my business coach. He is an amazing Facebook ads coach who has clients that are making 6 and 7 figures as a result of his coaching. He went on to tell me how he wasn't doing one weekly coaching call in his business anymore, he was doing two now. His clients fell in to two categories – those making 0-$20k and those making $20k to $30k. He was now putting them on separate calls based on their income levels.

I asked him why he separated his calls. I thought it was inspiring for clients who weren't making much money to listen to the more successful clients who were making a lot more money.

He told me it was having the opposite effect and that the lower income people were bringing down the higher income people – and that's when he decided to do separate calls.

If we are spending a lot of time with chronic complainers, martyrs, over-givers, people-pleasers and negative people, then it's going to be hard to change.

If we change our circle of influence, it will have a positive effect on your life.

Create a Sacred Circle of people who are committed to growth and healing. That's how you excel your progress. If you continue to hang out with the lower energy people, they will actually bring you down.

I want to thank you so much for reading my book! I hope it's helped you make some changes in your life.

I wish you all the best and take good *care* of yourself!

Michelle Kulp

Resources

- Meditation App – Chimes
- Emotional Healing Retreats – Jon Terrell of https://www.awakenment-wellness.com/
- Melissa Feick of www.melissafeick.com
- Nanci Deutsch of https://nancideutsch.com/
- *A Course in Miracles* by the Foundation for Inner Peace
- *The Surrender Experiment* by Michael Singer
- *A New Earth* by Eckhardt Tolle
- *Stillness is the Key* by Ryan Holiday
- *Quiet* by Susan Cain
- *Loving What Is* by Byron Katie

www.ingramcontent.com/pod-product-compliance
Lightning Source LLC
LaVergne TN
LVHW051847080426
835512LV00018B/3117